cabin, cottage & camp

new designs on the Canadian landscape

cabin, cottage & camp

new designs on the Canadian landscape

CHRISTOPHER MACDONALD

WITH CONTRIBUTIONS
BY HERBERT ENNS
AND PETER PRANGNELL

First published in 2005 by BLUE*m*PRINT

Book design by Elisa Gutiérrez

Printed and bound in Italy

Library and Archives Canada Cataloguing in Publication

Macdonald, Christopher A., 1953-
    Cabin, cottage and camp : new designs on the Canadian Landscape / Christopher A. Macdonald, Jana Tyner : contributions from Herbert Enns and Peter Prangnell.

ISBN 1-894965-30-2

    1. Vacation homes--Designs and plans. 2.--Designs and plans. I. Tyner, Jana, 1967- II.Title.

NA7579.C3M23 2005   728.7'2'0222   C2005-900581-5

Contents

'Landscapes can be deceptive.
Sometimes a landscape seems to
be less a setting for the life of its
inhabitants than a curtain behind
which their struggles, achievements
and accidents take place.
For those, who, with the inhabitants,
are behind the curtain, landscapes
are no longer only geographic but
also biographical and personal.'

John Berger in 'A Fortunate Man'

Cabin, cottage, camp...

Whether inhabited for a weekend or through the commitment of generations, these experiences are habitually given pride of place in our memory, often standing in stark contrast to hectic and media saturated lives.

1 Prior to establishing Taliesin West, Wright built the Ocotillo Desert Camp at nearby Chandler Arizona in the winter of 1929. Constructed as a base to work on a recent commission, the camp was 'abandoned in May when the heat became overbearing'. Gwendolyn Wright in 'Frank Lloyd Wright in the Domestic Landscape', 1994.

View of Ocotillo Camp in construction 30 January 1929. From page 26, Frank Lloyd Wright Selected Houses 3: Taliesin West, A.D.A. EDITA Tokyo Co. Ltd., Tokyo 1989.

2 This relationship is especially clear in the relatively benign climate of coastal British Columbia. In the example of the B.C. Binning house built in West Vancouver in 1941 these attributes find a fresh and complete expression. The sense of house-as-cabin could in this instance equally reference the house's built-in storage cabinets to the boat interiors familiar to Binning and his wife.

The words alone draw us into a realm in which intimate personal histories find themselves linked to the geographic complexity of a vast hinterland. The experience of an alternative home vividly engaged with season and situation draws a strong resonance across ages, regions and cultures. Private moments co-exist with the mythic constituents of a nation and offer lingering evocation of sensual, even primal settlement to our increasingly cosmopolitan and urban population.

Within the specific traditions of architectural culture, the discrete shelter immersed in its landscape setting has proved of enduring interest and at times seminal import. Whether Laugier's evocation of architecture's origins in the primitive hut, le Corbusier's côte d'Azur *cabanon* or Frank Lloyd Wright's winter camp at Scottsdale,[1] these structures stand as emblems of a particular realm of design attributes and intentions. Their typically direct expression and modest means contrive to depict those qualities in dwelling that might rightfully be considered *essential*.

Architecture's modern tradition - at least here in Canada - might even be reformulated as an effort to bring aspects of camp culture into the realm of mainstream domestic life. Informal planning of programme, literal engagement with adjacent landscapes, material economy and a direct expression of structure: all are attributes as easily ascribed to the cabin as they are to the early essays in a local modern idiom.[2]

The varied projects collected here represent the enduring value of a 'home away' in distilled and even poetic terms. Regardless of scale or situation, the projects' accomplishments are measured by their ability to conjure new habits of life and leisure and in so doing to expand the horizons of what we by habit consider to be *domestic*.

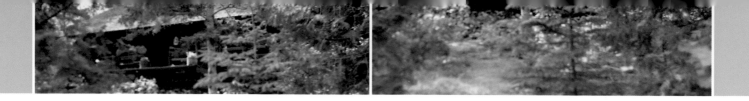

Cabin

In this question of how the conditions of locale are able to enliven the expectations of daily life we can find a clear indication of how the experience of cabin and camp can be rendered extraordinary.

3 One need only think of the kind of adjustments made to register highly local variations in climate - the favored deck for morning coffee, the room left vacant until rainy-day jigsaw puzzles appear, the inevitable screen door...

4 It is above all else this ability to operate as distilled, mnemonic for their surroundings that gives cabin and cottage their particular appeal and cultural currency.

A theme that recurs in many of the projects is the overlay of patterns of specific domestic lives with the defining structures of a surrounding landscape. The structures may be broad in definition - the watershed surrounding a lake, say - or described in terms of surface textures of the immediate site itself. Such an overlay can assume various tactics - intimate, expansive, reclusive, intertwined, disengaged - yet in each instance inarguable landforms present an immediate logic that is invited to the task of organizing the building site.

In the following works of *Ian MacDonald*, *Pierre Thibault* and *Patkau Architects*, the projects establish a clear sense of grounded identity while suggesting important relationships between the activities of the house and the outer world.[3] Carefully delineated local landscapes directly adjacent to interior spaces extend and often supplement the interior that surrounds the specific concerns of domestic life. Simultaneously, the positioning of the house within a much broader landscape serves to give a sense of priority to common living spaces.

The textures and physicality of both site and region are deeply implicated in these houses' organization. In this sense cabin and camp transcend their most obvious sense of destination: they manage to serve as a dense encapsulation of the landscape itself[4] brought into direct and daily contact with domestic life.

Ian MacDonald Architect Inc.

This project for a weekend country house and studio was designed with the potential for full-time residency in the future. The site - a 100-acre parcel of heavily treed land in the Mulmur Hills outside of Toronto - is remarkable for its dramatic topographical features and picturesque landscape.

The topographical complexity and dense tree cover of the existing site condition is both beautiful, and disorienting. Two geographical features in this landscape are sufficiently powerful that one's experience can be structured in relation to them: a north / south ridge that connects various remarkable valley and mature forest landscapes and a dramatic distant view to the Pine River Valley from the tip of a hilltop plateau. The house and its gardens connect these two important features with a visual axis and intermittent path defined along its length by architectural and landscape elements.

The axis serves as an armature through which one can understand and engage the site. At the west end, dramatic views over the valley landscape are framed by windows in the principle rooms of the house. At the east end, intimate views of a forested valley are captured from a prospect of quiet contemplation. The views at each end of the armature compliment each other and enhance one's appreciation of the rich and dramatic possibilities for experience of this special site. The sequence of discovery is controlled strategically by the careful design of the house and its garden.

The detailed nature of the place of the site is revealed incrementally, and its relationship to the larger world seems anchored and inevitable

13

Ian MacDonald

Ian MacDonald

15

IAN MACDONALD

19

Residence 'Les Abouts'

PIERRE THIBAULT ARCHITECTE

A country house designed for art collectors, this work is located in the St. Lawrence Lowlands adjacent to a river and dominated by a dense pine forest. The landform is characteristic of the region, formed by slow erosion of the river. The site is accessible across a gentle grade to a wooded plateau.

The plan is displayed with flexibility under three distinct parts: a private zone, a public zone and - between the two - an area of circulation. The more private family area includes master bedroom and bathroom, the kitchen and a shared bathroom. The generous fenestration offers brightness and permeability to those spaces and opens onto a large peripheral porch. The indoor/outdoor harmony is supported by a veranda (adjoining the kitchen overhanging the ferns) and a winter garden.

The public zone includes living room, a library and guest rooms. This large two-storey volume provides the receptacle for works of art. Guest rooms and a library shape the space. The rooms are hung from the roof in a cubic volume and the circular library is perched up on steel stilts. Wooden post and beam and timber-frame walls are used, allowing for the clerestory framing walls and providing warmth and mellowness, inside as well as out.

PIERRE THIBAULT

23

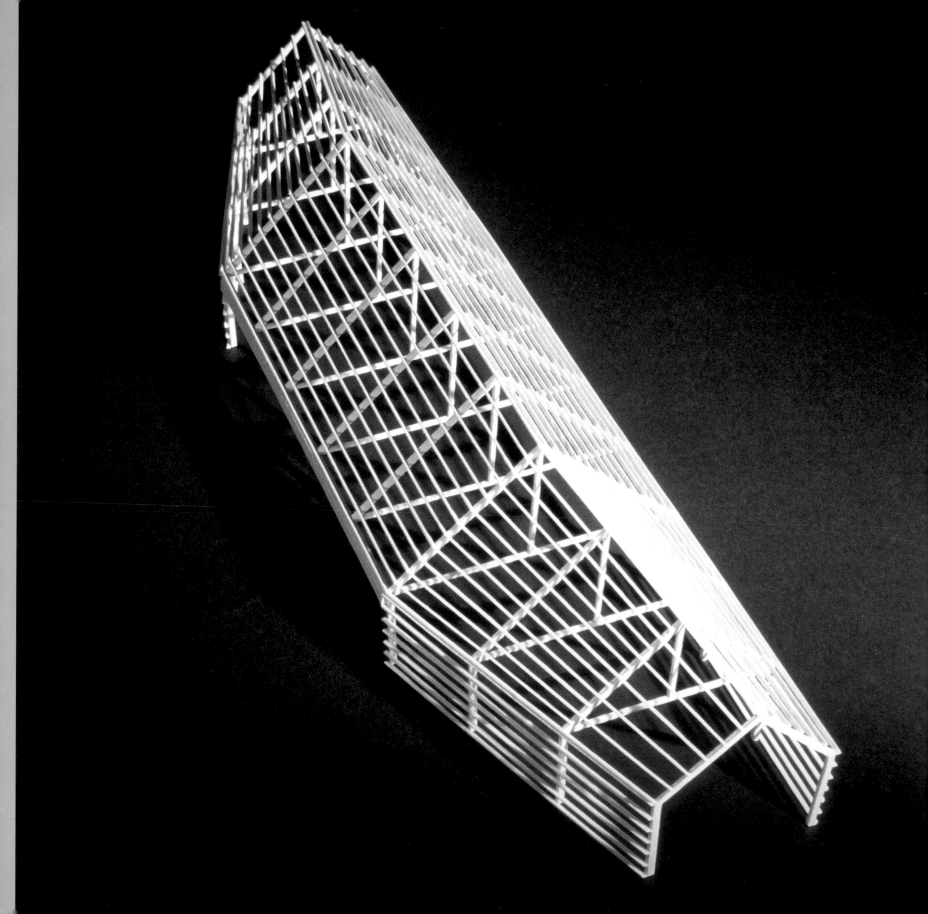

Port Cunnington Cottage

PATKAU ARCHITECTS

This small cottage was designed to sit within a forest setting on a rocky ledge overlooking the Lake of Bays in northern Ontario. It is approached on foot along the rock ridge and entered from the back facing the lake.

The cottage consists of a common living space flanked at either end by self-contained bedroom suites. The bedroom organization is meant to accommodate a range of possible occupants... a family with children, two couples, a couple along with their married children, etc. Extra beds will be available!

The form of the building is a simple shed that has been warped slightly. The wooden framing members and sheathing are exposed to the interior much like the interior of a wooden canoe. The exterior is clad with a soft gray metal so that it will sit quietly within the forest setting.

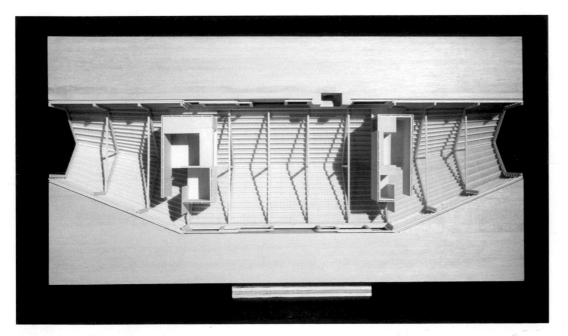

Countryside

When such a sensibility is
granted sufficient terrain and
low density of settlement -
qualities that fortunately occur
in abundance in the Canadian
hinterland - the urge for refuge
can be rendered sublime.

Within the lexicon of geographic variation that attracts recreational use, the unfettered view of uninhabited landscape is persistently dominant. Conventional acknowledgement of the manners of the street is countered by the spatial release of an expansive view as a determining focus of the plan. This literal representation of dwelling as an experience removed from society and heavily invested in the passive, visual regard for landscape presents a *motif* that is often very directly inscribed into the organization of both plan and section. Particularly when set in an environment of modest dimension, this inclination places direct pressure on the organization of a domestic programme, since the condition of directional bias underpins all other decisions.

Whether in the two waterfront locations of projects by *Peter Cardew* and *Battersby-Howat* or *Florian Maurer's* assembly of pavilions perched on an escarpment, such structures enjoy the precipitous condition of a geographical edge as the point of fissure between everyday life and the repose of the cottage. Here in particular the orchestration of approach is finely considered as a prolonged and delicate moment of transition that is as much social as it is spatial. The culmination of arrival in the expansive view of distant landscape is in each case forcefully stated by the dimension and logic of an organizing structural frame.

BATTERSBYHOWAT

The project was designed for clients who wished to build a part-time retirement home. In the initial meeting, they presented images of Philip Johnson's Glass House as an expression of their desire for sophistication and simplicity.

The site is a half-acre waterfront lot located on one of the Southern Gulf Islands in the Straight of Georgia, west of Vancouver. Mature arbutus, cedar, and fir trees open to reveal glimpses of the water beyond, while the arid climate of the island supports limited undergrowth below. The dwelling is organized in response to the particular conditions of its site and context, as well as its method of production and construction. The resulting architecture is as much a pragmatic response as it is an intuitive reaction to the project's defining parameters.

Opaque north and east elevations are flanked by public roadways. Concrete and stucco are used both literally as foundation and conceptually as anchors, embedding the project in its context. Conversely, yellow cedar cladding is employed at direct points of inhabitation - entries, decks, and at the terrace adjacent to the western façade - providing sympathetic scale and materiality.

In contrast to the predominantly enigmatic expression of the north elevation, the west and south elevations are view-oriented and dominated by glazing and framed construction, cantilevering above the site and detailed to articulate their constituent parts.

As an extension of previous and ongoing investigations by the firm's office, this project explores the potential to derive significant architectural expression from seemingly prosaic means.

29

BATTERSBYHOWAT

31

33

35

FLORIAN MAURER ARCHITECT INC.

Site motivated the design for this house in B.C.'s South Okanagan, providing an opportunity to experiment with the construction of open space set within interior buildings reminiscent of Latin-inspired traditions of interior courtyards. A group of ponderosa pines in the centre of the site encouraged the creation of a small 'village' around the cluster of trees, separating the building functions into components.

The studio and the single car garage form a gateway through which everyone must walk to reach the inner garden and the main building. The main house is built on a ridge of bedrock with views of Okanagan Lake to the west, and the tranquility of the sheltered garden to the east. The master bedroom is a separate pavilion to the southeast, creating a private patio together with the main house and the bedrock ridge. Because mature trees close to the northern border precluded closing the courtyard with building components, a dense forest of russian olive trees has been planted to visually enclose the space.

The fragile underpinning of our national culture and its shallow historical frame is rendered intimate and palpable as it is shared around a campfire.

The South Okanagan is a semi-arid area with dry, hot summers and moderate, cloudy winters. The lot rises gently to a bedrock outcrop, where it drops steeply. Issues of sustainability and a direct response to this climate and site were addressed in numerous ways. Placement of buildings, size and location of roof overhangs and existing mature trees, performance of glazing product, thermal capacity of concrete slab and tile flooring, all worked together to reduce heat gain in summer.

The clump of ponderosa pines on both sides of the building offer shade and bird habitat, while the afternoon lake breeze blowing through the house from west to east makes air conditioning unnecessary.

FLORIAN MAURER

39

41

43

Camp

The fragile underpinning of our national culture and its shallow historical frame is rendered intimate and palpable as it is shared around a campfire.

5 A particular evocation of dwelling as campsite is made by Rudolf Schindler in his Los Angeles home of 1922: 'The plan was based on the principle of their campsite at Yosemite Park - a solid wall at the back and light screen at the front.' Esther McCoy in 'Vienna to Los Angeles: Two Journeys', 1979.

View of garden from Pauline Schindler room, Schindler-Chase residence, Hollywood Road, Los Angeles. From page 20, Zubmann: Schindler, Zero Editions, Santa Monica, 1996.

The expression *camp* holds a particularly suggestive - if somewhat archaic - meaning in the context of the work included here. Certainly it should be ascribed to a collection of structures, with the implicit sense of a larger community and likely an accompanying history. Yet the word also reminds us that the construction of settlement is, in the Canadian colonial context, just barely removed from *campsite*,[5] *fish-camp, logging camp...*

   The provisional attitude of seasonal occupation represents not only a recent pattern of leisure activity but also the habit and necessity of occupying the land and bringing it into productive mode. This reminder that collective histories begin in immediate action amplifies the regard for aspects of site, geography and material culture noted here.

   In the powerful description of his own family's camp on an island in Ontario's Shoal Lake that follows, architect *Herbert Enns* reveals the full gamut of emotional and material investment that *settlement* is capable of. The project variously serves as emblem of the geological order of the Canadian Shield, deliberate logics of geometry and construction, an acknowledged passage of season and moment, the inevitable collusion of visual and haptic pleasures, traces of historic human presence on the land - and *more...*

   Here is record of an ongoing proposition for living that is truly rich and rare.

HERBERT ENNS

The *Experimental Buildings* are really two modest pavilions constructed in stages on a remote island in Shoal Lake, which straddles the Manitoba/Ontario border. The extremely low budget is made possible through the use of low-cost and recycled materials (including windows from the renovated Russell Building at the University of Manitoba), and efficient modes of construction. The architect is the builder. The interior of the main pavilion accommodates living, cooking, dining and guest sleeping space; the secondary pavilion provides sleeping for four.

The buildings are temporary and evolving, constructed of wood foundations to contrast with the permanence of stone. A skylight slices through the building at a 12-degree angle, oriented to the North Star. Walls, doors and operable panels open in summer to transform the structure into a building of screens and natural ventilation.

The main pavilion is aligned with the shoreline and oriented to prominent views. It becomes an observatory of the changing skies and seasons.

The north elevation is the closed 'back' of the building, providing protection from the prevailing winds. The south elevation is an 'open' façade with five recycled windows and an 8'x8' sliding wall. The east elevation is clad in translucent corrugated fibreglass panels that diffuse light and reveal the structural wood frame. A herringbone pattern of diagonal bracing stiffens the frame.

The main pavilion is aligned with the shoreline and oriented to prominent views. It becomes an observatory of the changing skies and seasons.

HERBERT ENNS

49

HERBERT ENNS

Places are registered in the psyche. They are in us. When we acquire even the most modest external out-of-context stimuli, we are instantly transported to another place. The smell of 2-cycle engine exhaust transports me immediately to the motor rickshaws on the streets of New Delhi, as quickly as clear air brings me back to a Canadian winter, or pine scent to Shoal Lake. What wells up in us is the sense of a tactile and visceral place - fully dimensional, fully coloured, fully real.

Violence & Mercy / Black & White

by Herbert Enns

The Experimental Buildings At Shoal Lake 11.01.05

These writings illuminate the Experimental Buildings at Shoal Lake, where pragmatism and spirituality coexist. They also shed light on a multi-layered architecture that operates as filter, transitive element, social condenser and ultralight place marker. The expectations for the project are high, and the means modest. They are derived from a set of beliefs, priorities and choices that define a distinct lifestyle outside of the conventional patterns of everyday life, and everyday architecture. Unusual in time frame, an extended reflective context for architectural experimentation is a rare commodity. The Experimental Buildings at Shoal Lake are a philosophical, perceptual, social and technical test bed for architecture. Following the purchase in 1987 of one-half of a 24-acre island, the two small pavilions have been constructed in stages over the summers beginning in 1995, and these are the subject of the Cabin + Camp contribution.

   Writing about the buildings is an elusive endeavour. Architecture exists *in situ* and beyond text, a space for the soul (Jung) - to be imagined, to be built, to be inhabited, and to be re-imagined in infinite ways. When the artists who I admire - Agnes Martin, Richard Serra, Robert Irwin, James Turrell, Donald Judd - write or speak about their work, they are straightforward and unencumbered by jargon. The highest achievements in abstract art are most often described with distilled directness and clarity - the outcome, one imagines, of considerable thought. This text is a deliberate construction - a constructed syntactical meditation. Like the landscape and projects, the writings have colour and scale: first, as big as the world - a broad historical spectrum, the macro context, the meta-organizing structure - and then (now), collapsing into the micro near-sighted landscape - where the hammer meets the nail and where everything is black and white.

A

A is for Africa. A is *in* Africa: A (Africa) is (in) the body of the essay, in the body of the buildings. On Christmas Eve, 1986, Maem Slater-Enns and I arrive in Winnipeg following twenty-four hours of slingshot-flights originating in Nairobi, Kenya. One minute we were sitting amongst flowering Jacaranda trees under African skies, the next we were attending midnight mass on Christmas Eve at St. Margaret's

Anglican Church, Ethelbert and Westminster. In the preceding three months we had camped along the Sand River in the Serengeti borderlands of Tanzania and Kenya; wandered through the organized chaos of New and Old Delhi; and trekked up to Manang at 4,000 meters altitude, into the Annapurna Himal of Nepal. We had traveled to Ethiopia to observe the aftermath of the 1985 famine - the country still in shock, fighting a civil war, and in the grips of a dictator. In Kenya, we took the overnight train that runs north of Kilamanjaro from Nairobi down to Mombasa, visiting Malindi and Lamu on the Indian Ocean.

The trip opened our eyes: it helped us to see outside of ourselves. And on that twenty-four hour race with the sun to get home for Christmas, we decided - among other things - that acquiring open land in the Canadian wilderness was a unique possibility - freedom of choice and opportunity equated with space, wilderness, and water in abundance. Canada was the promised land, we realized. The rest is history ... and out of our hands. One thing led to another (or perhaps we were led to one thing and then to another). The island on Shoal Lake - displacing, transcending, separating, extending, and gathering - is every place we have ever been. *Agnes Martin, the minimalist painter, said that first you must find the place, and then you can decide what to do in that place.* A is for Africa.

X

X marks the spot. X is where and who and what ... X Y Z. X = 95° 04' W, Y = 49° 34' N, and Z = 1077.0 feet (322.8 metres) above sea level. 49° 34' is also the angle of incline to the North Star - its azimuth. This is what I mean by north, north with an axis - polar, not magnetic - true north, looking up. The slice through the roof of the living/dining pavilion is north/south. Blue-white North Star sky-space. We lie on the hard maple floor in August and watch the stars pivot.

X is the multiplication symbol (times). I like to compare the building's anticipated life span to the site lifespan - an 80-year building/human life will span a 2.5 billion year geological history 31,500,000 times. 80 x 31,500,000 lifetimes = 2,500,000,000, the age of the stone islands of Shoal Lake. I made the buildings temporary, with wood foundations to contrast the most permanent material on earth. They are largely made of organic matter, like the overburden that grips the roots of Saskatoon and chokecherry bushes, American yew, and white pine.

X is also the cross bracing - a herringbone (pickerelbone) bracing of spruce threaded into the building frames to resist lateral forces. A sense of structure is the highest order of architectural instinct. I capitalized the X, to emphasize that beauty in the eye (/) and beauty in the heart (\ ) needs a connection to the landscape that is bigger than the eye and the heart combined. Criss / Cross. I wanted the buildings to approach a state of vulnerability, to emphasize the effects of time and weather and wind. *'This building is shaking,'* Benedikt said, with his hand on the pickerelbone braced frame. *'No, that's impossible,'* I replied. A blast of cold late September northwest wind vibrated through the structure. Denial - like an instinct for structure - is an important architectural device.

Notes

i Lake of the Woods Northwestern Portion: Ptarmigan Bay and Shoal Lake; Scale 1:40,000; surveyed by the Canadian Hydrographic service, 1968-69; © Minister of Fisheries and Oceans Canada, 1987. (Map 6217)

ii 12' x 24' + 16" o/c (floor joists, wall studs and roof joists)
+ 8' x 8' sheathing (9 module floor/ 12 module roof)
+ 12° roof slope
+ 32" over 144" (a 2 bay shift in plan to orient sky pace to the North Star)
+ 4" framing - 32" = 24" x 156" parallelogram is the sky slice
+ 8' x 8' opening (void) displaced in south wall
+ 8' x 8' wall (solid) shifted north and rotated 12° at entry
+ 6 operable panels
+ 2 doors
+ 8 - 2' x 5' fixed glazing units reclaimed from the J. A. Russell Building
+ 1959 date stamp in the sealed units
+ 2" x 4" milled cedar window frames
+ 1 1/4" x 1/8" aluminum stops
+ 16 - 1" flathead stainless steel screws countersunk in aluminum

+

The 6217 [i] map of the lake has '+' marking the shoals - where granite meets aluminum prop all too often. Shoal Lake, on the Manitoba / Ontario border is a largely uninhabited 277 square kilometer lake. It contains 2.64 billion cubic liters of fresh water and usually drains into Lake of the Woods at Ash Rapids. (The current at Ash Rapids can reverse itself, depending on rainfall and runoff. It is an artificial channel blasted with dynamite.) This pristine body of water has been preserved from intense development to protect Winnipeg's water intake at the head of Indian Bay. Winnipeg is licensed to drain up to 455 million liters of water per day from the lake through a 150 kilometer aqueduct. H2O - the life-code around which the modern world will revolve - as far as the eye can see.

The '+' sign is the cruciform in every mathematical formula ever derived. It links the tangled geometry in every calculation for the *mathematics of the ideal villa*. There is a mathematical coherence and consistency in the modularity of the plan. The integration of structure, construction systems, and form are mathematically derived. The most ephemeral attributes in light architecture are products of reason:

$$12' \times 24' + 16" \text{ o/c} + 8 \times 8 \ (9 + 12) + 12° + 32" \ / \ 144" + 4" - 32" = 24" \times$$
$$156" + 8' \times 8' + 8' \times 8' \ 12° + 6 + 2 + 8 - 2' \times 5' + 1959 + 2" \times 4" + 1 \ 1/4"$$
$$\times 1/8" + 16 - 1" \ [ii]$$

These intricate geometries and proportioning ratios are an embedded logic that governs the connections between uncomplicated pieces, merging structure, span, construction methods, modular components, and prefabricated components with orientation and spatial proportioning. The numbers constitute a set of nested values and ratios to describe the array of ordinary pieces of wood, glass, aluminum, fiberglass, and rubber: like a profound text of simple words. Transcendent perception is rooted in logic. At Shoal Lake the light is scaled as well. Each cedar window frame is handmade to a ratio of 2 to 5 to hold the double glazed units recycled from the John A. Russell Building at the University of Manitoba with the 1959 date stamp in the seal.

T

A crossed T is the crucifixion in every text I ever read and every text I ever wrote. Writers play God every day of their lives and so do 'A'rchitects. Some architects shy away from spirituality, but play God. Some architects play spirituality, but shy away from God - unnerved by the escape from violence that a beauty outside of themselves brings, for them/us violence is beautiful enough. The new brutality is in. I wanted to escape from violence to beauty. This is why the buildings are small - to minimize violence and amplify beauty. This is why the buildings pay so little regard to formal coherence - eight facades, two roofs and two floors add up to twelve different attempts to find the beauty that is outside of ourselves/myself ... this why they don't conform.

C/SEE

Cabin + Camp: that forceful letter C in the word *Construction* - its sound not its form - is like the sound of the C in the word *Cut* - like dragging a saw through spruce or fir. To cut douglas fir plywood - to cut down a douglas fir tree, to clear cut first growth forest, to cut down the coastal range - in order to configure a place of serenity in the wild is barbaric, unsophisticated, primitive, and violent. Construction is violent in almost every possible dimension. Some think it to be the spiritual essence of architecture. I do not. Its violence may be natural and necessary - a natural violence... a natural function of nature - but at incalculable costs that exceed the intentions and comprehensions we bring to the table.

In this entropic age, the consumption of the environment for our gratification represents the highest order of planetary violence, be it oil or wood or aluminum or clean air. This violation of the world is inescapable: a road of no return that we are all on, and we cannot help but participate in it as individuals by degree. The coated nail driven into a spruce floor joist is a subset of larger actions: a violence of necessity, less gratuitous than destroying the rainforest, but nevertheless connected. It is a personal single-handed act of aggression, an intimate violence. Thankfully, violence is scalable. I made the buildings small, using as many recycled materials as possible. First comes necessity, then comes morality: a stand-alone off-the-grid solar energy system for power and light further reduces the scale of construction/destruction violence. When the batteries run down at night, we go to bed. How much did the buildings cost? We had a small budget. We paid for them in cash. Is this what you mean? Or how much did they really cost? Who knows?

This is the architect's paradox. We employ violent acts of construction, seek the advent of mercy and emancipation *by* landscape, finding stillness in the world by will power, brute force, and physical strength. We build gossamer walls washed with light to save our souls. It all begins with a cut, a tree cut, saw cut, a cut to the eye. C in the *body* of the text is the cut in my cornea when the sliding translucent light-wall dropped from its mount and I tried to lift its 200 pound self out of the bush, back onto the silver coloured *Cannonball* door hardware that farmers like because its round profile is self-cleaning. The Teflon bearings last forever, but not the cornea (yours and mine). These cells take a long time to grow back - in fact they never fully heal. Picture this - the one-eyed architect carrying the weight of the transparent operable wall stumbling into a sharpened spear-like branch along the newly cleared path the kids cut through the bush to get to their 'kitchen' hideout.

iii http://collections.ic.gc.ca/ nativeterans/treatyareas/treaty _area3.htm

iv Native Communites within Treaty Number Three: Assabaska, Allenwater, Big Grassy, Big Island, Brokenhead, Couchiching, Dalles, Dinorwic, Dryden, Eagle Lake, Eagle River, Fort Alexander, Fort Frances, Frenchman's Head, Grassy Narrows, Hungry Hall, Islington, Keewatin, Kenora, Lac La Croix, Lac Seul, Long Sault No. 1, Long Sault No. 2, Manitou - Buffalo Point, Manitou Rapids, Morson, Northwest Angle, Onegaming, Rainy River, Rat Portage, Savanne, Savant Lake, Seine River, Shoal Lake #39, Shoal Lake #40, Sioux Lookout, Vermillion Bay, Wabigoon, White-dog, Whitefish Bay.

v Davidson-Hunt, I. and F. Berkes. 2003. Learning As You Journey: Anishinaabe Perception Of Social-Ecological Environ-ments And Adaptive Learning. Conservation Ecology 8(1): 5.

TP / T3

Treaty Number 3 was entered into by the First Nations living in the western portion of Ontario (north-west of Thunder Bay) and Queen Alexandrina Victoria - Queen of England, Ruler of the British Empire (1819-1901). Adhesions to the treaty were made in 1874. The treaty lands ranged from the United States border west to the Manitoba border from which it traces the watershed line midway through northern Ontario to near Lake Nipigon. The treaty is officially entitled, 'Treaty 3 between Her Majesty the Queen and the Saulteaux Tribe of the Ojibwa Indians at the Northwest Angle on the Lake of the Woods with Adhesions.' [iii] [iv] This treaty followed explorations by Verandrye in 1732. His eldest son, Sieur de la Verandrye was ambushed returning through Lake of the Woods in 1736.

Massacre Island remains unidentified, a footnote in history that underscores the entry of this water-way into the western lexicon of wild places. Presumably their ghosts still haunt the lake. We believe we own the land. We hold title to Mining Location JO 180. But the land has a contested history. I have never been comfortable with the idea of permanent ownership. We are fourth in the 'Course of Empire' line. The Founding Nations, the Crown, the staked claims of the gold miners, and the land speculator preceded us. What do the band members think when we haul boatload after boatload of material past the sacred island and exhaust ourselves to frame a strange subsistence in the middle of nowhere...on the edge of white land...in the centre of their existence. I built the buildings to be temporary - of the moment. [v]

We have found the essence of the Experimental Buildings to reside in complex non-architectural trajectories and strata. I like Patricia Reed's titles for her *Aesthetic Management* projects. She developed two pieces at *Akademie Schloss Solitude in 2004: A Space Traversed by Signals and Intermingled Geometries*. Reed monitors the space between, the non-figurative, the implied not the actual. The Experimental Buildings are like that. Their core life resides in - and is appreciated at - alternative levels.

Visitors to the project may have their own interpretation. For me, they exert a profound impact on our spatial perception and their role as waypoints is central to an expanding range of motion that encompasses increasingly extensive regions of Shoal Lake. In this sense they reinforce the gradual perceptual advance of what might be described as an *indigenous* response to landscape. Our departure from 'normal' routines and spatial/functional conventions affect our social cognition. The ever expanding lexicon of seasonal and climatic impacts weighs significantly on perception, inspiration and matters of safety - and indeed, survival. Finally, the all pervasive inescapability of our transitory and temporal existence - when contrasted with the incomprehensibility and vastness of the sky (read universe), the impenetrability of the stone islands, and the infinite colourations of northern lake light - describe the space of a paradox.

Places are registered in the *psyche*. They are in us. When we acquire even the most modest external out-of-context stimuli, we are instantly transported to another place. The smell of 2-cycle engine exhaust transports me immediately to the motor rickshaws on the streets of New Delhi, as quickly as clear air brings me back to a Canadian winter, or pine scent to Shoal Lake. What wells up in us is the sense of a tactile and visceral place - fully dimensional, fully coloured, fully real.

It is easy to mimic this strange removal and recall. Remember waking up from a strange hallucinatory place, grateful to escape fear as one wakes up in one's own room. The mind disassociates itself from context often. And when it does, we are momentarily blinded, perceptually unhinged from context. We are displaced by psychological and neurological means. This is why I painted the minimal hybrid murals, the most recent addition to the Experimental Buildings at Shoal Lake. Half architecture and half art, I was thinking about Ellsworth Kelly and Donald Judd when I painted pure black and pure white on douglas fir 3/4 G1S plywood panels. A visual baseline to mark the point of departure and the point of return - no colour/all colours, the beginning and the end, alpha and omega, black and white.

The contrast in Herbert Enns' work between the spareness of the constructed elements and the evident fullness of the camp's meaning and value should not go unmarked. It is precisely here that traditions of an economy of means and directness of expression have been recognized and brought into their particular repose. In this instance the project not only serves as distilled rendering of landscape but also as an endlessly expansive record of passionate human experience. This ability to be markedly singular while retaining a provisional character represents the high degree of measure that a decidedly contemporary expression might bring to the cabin and camp undertaking.

It is also pertinent to consider the traditions of abstraction and modernity alluded to in Enns' writing. The projects collected here conspicuously sidestep literal allusion to vernacular type and historicist language. They do so while retaining clear resonances with the experience of traditional forms and the social values and material cultures that accompanied their production. The work consistently declares virtues of sentiment while avoiding sentimentality, and if the word modern appears insufficient it would be fair to recognize a common sense of optimism.

It is this quality - the works' collective sense of anticipation - that has more than anything drawn them together in this current miscellany.

Caban

In each case, an overarching interest in 'paring back' refreshes our sense of how to live modestly in the world while serving as design laboratory and source of inspiration.

6 Le Corbusier's own *cabanon* of 1951 was sixteen square metres in area, according to its author: 'Not a square centimetre wasted! A little cell at human scale where all functions were considered'.

Common to countryside retreats and the traditions of modern architecture is a recurring fascination with the proposition of a minimal dwelling.[6]

This concern for the minimal represents the desire for a realm in which a culture's sometimes overbearing articulation of shelter can be restrained - indeed reduced to the point at which the world could be experienced in a virtual state of grace. In so doing, the project of reduced means holds the capacity to draw our attention to that which is *essential*, a hugely beneficial quality in a living environment intended as retreat and repose: as *antidote*.

In the caban by *Pierre Thibault*, the condition of ad-hoc construction common to cottage traditions is clearly registered. Nothing more or less than an assembly of impulse, the project nonetheless establishes a clear sense of orientation, delineation of programme and offers a symbolic presence in the landscape.

Two much more considered works bring another level of material refinement to circumstances of modest dimension and intent. 'La Petite Maison du Weekend' by *Patkau Architects* includes interests in environmental sustainability and the potential of the country dwelling to be a complete manufactured item. A small guest house also used to stage parties designed by *Shim-Sutcliffe* locates the sublime components of the cottage milieu in a highly sophisticated and urbane landscape setting.

Habitats Légers

PIERRE THIBAULT ARCHITECTE

Constructed in a village near Quebec City, this life-sized prototype for a very simple and inexpensive refuge draws inspiration from its setting and vernacular constructions. An entirely horizontal space anchored in the landscape, with one long band of windows alongside the space for sleeping and eating and another space completely open to the exterior for everything else: the desire to offer as much as possible within a minimal format in order to change one's perception of time.

This project most directly exemplifies the ethos of casual construction associated with cottage culture. In its improvised plan and decidedly *ad hoc* assembly, the house resembles a constructed sketch provisionally positioned for an indeterminate future.

La Petite Maison du Weekend

Patkau Architects

This prototypical recreational house was designed and built as part of a competition sponsored by the Wexner Center for the Arts in Columbus, Ohio. The project is conceived as a portable, self-contained dwelling that could be placed in any outdoor site. The dwelling unit provides the basics of habitation for two, and includes a loft bed, a kitchen, and a bathroom with a composting toilet. Electricity is self-generated, while rainwater is collected and reused.

Patkau

Ravine Guest House and Reflecting Pool

SHIM-SUTCLIFFE ARCHITECTS

This modern guest house and reflecting pool is located on the grounds of a residence abutting a Toronto ravine. It is conceived of as an open pavilion sitting in a lush verdant landscape.

A wood burning indoor/outdoor fireplace plays a pivotal role in the project. It acts as the centre of the pavilion, tying the enclosed interior space with the covered but open deck beyond. It has an operable fire glass window between the two sides creating reflections and views from one space to the other. A pair of double doors allows the entire glazed wall of this guest house to open to the pool deck beyond. When completely open, the indoor and outdoor spaces flow together creating ambiguity between inside and outside.

The programme consists of both indoor and outdoor elements. The indoor programme includes a sitting room with sleeping area, a kitchen suitable for the guest house as well as serving for catering large parties, and a bathroom. The outdoor programme includes a large wooden deck, reflecting pool with water lilies, bullrushes and fish, an outdoor covered dining area, with a long concrete countertop for big parties with wood storage below and a lower level with storage for garden equipment.

Cottage

The results express a degree of
intimacy and character rarely
encountered in the world of
calculated and resolved design.

A curious condition of much Canadian agrarian hinterland is its oblique representation in structures with direct industrial affinities. Storage sheds that measure a quarter-section of forage - or its equivalent herd of cattle - stand as isolated and silent witnesses to the land's cultivation. These structures bear an undeniable sense of purpose even when - to the uninformed visitor at least - that purpose remains inscrutable.

Set in deliberate acknowledgement of its agricultural neighbours in this regard, the Hobby House project of *Peter Prangnell* and *Tony Belcher* appears on its approach to literally hover above its surrounding meadow. The house quietly commands its immediate domain while enjoying views of broader dimension. Anticipating at least occasional occupation during winter months, the house's organization is also inflected in deference to seasonal weather patterns.

Within, another sort of cultivation is evoked in which confidence and unwavering commitment are exercised over time. This evocation of how a process - a life - is engaged in the creation of a modest home in the countryside speaks directly to the need to accompany intent with affection and is given eloquent voice in Prangnell's essay that follows. The project as well speaks to architectural traditions in which incident and occasion are given privilege, a sensibility well suited to the tactic of staged intervention on which the construction was founded.

Hobby House, Euphrasia

PETER PRANGNELL AND ANTHONY BELCHER

A house designed and largely built for its architect owners - Tony Belcher and Peter Prangnell - the Hobby House is situated on a pastoral ten-acre field about two hours' drive from Toronto. The situation includes distinct topographical shape including south facing slopes and long views to the east, south and west.

The project was designed with an anticipation of sequential stages of construction, beginning with a central portion that would have everything necessary to be comfortable for a weekend and be heated to prevent pipes freezing. A *cabanon* in Canada. Larger spaces - constructed in two subsequent stages - were designed to be used primarily in the summer. Their use was to be forfeited in winter except on special occasions when drained pipes could be filled and stoves would be lit. These spaces would, in turn, help insulate and protect the central space from the general nastiness of Canadian winters.

The extended period of simultaneous design, construction and use - rather than on a period of use after the nominal completion of a building - suggests a series of 'interventions', accommodating evolving concerns and pragmatic necessities.

The extended period of simultaneous design, construction and use - rather than on a period of use after the nominal completion of a building - suggests a series of 'interventions', accommodating evolving concerns and pragmatic necessities.

Hobby House

BY PETER PRANGNELL

ORIGINALLY PUBLISHED IN EXTENDED FORM IN SPAZIO E SOCIETÀ XXII, N. 92 (OCT-DEC 2000).

I have to conclude that architects, like all who vainly attempt to stem its inevitable effects, willfully ignore the benefits of time. Restorations and face-lifts proceed apace. I understand that even in Le Corbusier's Pessac housing project one house has been restored by its owners and is listed as a *Monument Historique*. Albeit slowly, other houses are being returned by enthusiastic householders, to their 'original' state. There is much irony in this: just as architects came to terms with the changes house-holders made to the original buildings, they now have to change tack and contradict Le Corbusier. You may recall that he declared 'You know, it is always life that is right and the architect who is wrong'.

At the time, it was taken to be a generous, though perhaps rueful, acknowledgement of the effect of time and people on his work. For a short time in some architectural circles, it was accepted that people who used buildings might feel free to adapt them - fine tune them, that is, to needs and idio-syncrasies that went beyond the purview of their architects. (Of course, in some other circles, it was still assumed that people had to adapt to architects' buildings.)

Not so long ago, a few architects suggested that their mission (forgive the word) was to initiate concepts that were able to receive predictable, and often not so predictable, interpretations as their buildings came to be used. Architects generally do not take so kindly to the interventions (forgive the word) that may be willed, or as they would have it, wreaked, on their work. Tony Belcher and I have been trying to deal with a variety of 'interventions' as we worked our way through designing and building a house for ourselves.

It has taken seventeen years so far - and we are not quite done yet. Our experiment in time has focused on an extended period of simultaneous design, construction and use (rather than on a period of use after the nominal completion of a building). Our responsibilities were complicated by being architects, builders and users, all at the same time. We have had time to realize that latent in any design is its potential for changes. Which is exactly what buildings have latent in them, like it or not. No 'frozen music' after all!

In 1986 we had bought ten acres - a field with distinct topographical shape, south facing slopes and long views to the east, south and west, about two hours' drive from our Toronto home. We embraced the local habit of weekending in the country. 'Going to the cottage,' as it is known here, is changing

Notes

i An alternative way of a thing being 'all of a piece' would be if it was an exact response to, or reflection of, 'inhabitation' as, for example, birds' nests are - shaky ground for designers, smacking of 'natural' determinism, though, on reflection, no less shaky than, say, the 'commodificational' determinism of most 'down to the teaspoons' design strategies. Neither strategy allows much leeway for change or improvement.

from the seasonal accommodation of camps (as the upper middle class referred to their compounds of Spartan cabins) to year-round retreats that, apart from a veneer of rusticity, duplicate the amenities of the city. Knowing we would build in stages, we developed a compromise: the central part (stage 1) of our house would have everything necessary for us to be comfortable for a weekend and be heated to prevent pipes freezing. A *cabanon* in Canada. Larger spaces (stages 2 and 3) would be used primarily in the summer. We would forfeit their use in winter except on special occasions when we would fill drained pipes and light stoves. These spaces would, in turn, help insulate and protect the central space from the general nastiness of Canadian winters.

With this much of a programme decided, we made a drawing which, as most drawings do, emphasized graphic qualities of our ideas rather than our abilities as builders. The emphasis of graphic elements seduces us into believing that the problem has been contained, that we've licked the chaotic world into a neat, comprehensive form. We did this with an oval, quite literally giving an eggshell form to a yolk-like core. With some sleight-of-hand, we juggled axes, skewing and, later, slipping them, and generally complicating their geometries. An overlay of lines suggested spaces of more and of less importance, a tentative structure and an allusion to rhythm. It was a way of getting a thing to look as if it was 'all of a piece' - a discrete or finite thing. Being so 'suitable for framing', however, it inhibited its own development or metamorphosis.[i]

Our first design took advantage of the south-facing slope having a forty feet by twenty feet basement laid across the contours with the twenty feet by twenty feet *cabanon* on its north end. The basement roof, extended from the *cabanon*, provided a deck and a plunge pool. On either side curved wings formed the summer spaces: on the east a bedroom and on the west a living room. We drew the *cabanon* and its basement support as a core of masonry protected by the wings of lightweight framing. The *cabanon* set on the basement was to use a new masonry product which gave good insulation and was capable of supporting a concrete vaulted roof which would carry a sloping, grassed roof which rose up out of the meadow to an overlook. The entrance to the house was to be to one side of the sloping roof, at the level of a loft (or mezzanine) in the wing on the west side. The roof is significant for two reasons: it was an attempt to interpret the geography of the land 'poetically' and it belied our enthusiasm for local agricultural buildings.[ii]

Our enthusiasm for agricultural buildings was to be laid on our work quite literally. We admired their arrangements of discrete pieces and their materials (the metal siding or the timber framing). Above all, as buildings they came as close as buildings can be to being 'matter-of-fact.' (If not quite as intensely 'matter-of-fact' as any piece dubbed '*objet type*' by Le Corbusier). We saw in them qualities and conditions that coincided with our interests: their purpose was direct and simple, as was their construction; like many industrial buildings, ostentation, if apparent at all, is no more than a grace-note, a flourish of enthusiasm; and most important, their relationship with the landscape is direct. Paying homage to them, we tried to make our house as if it was a generic product, resisting, as much as we could, kneading the design into an object of commodity aesthetics.[iii]

As we began construction, we quickly realized how far out of our depth we were. To make things simpler, we realized the basement floor to the level of an 'undercroft' beneath the west wing. An open areaway behind it on the north made a path down to the 'undercroft.' The concrete vaults were replaced with timber joists. In turn, the timber joist construction made for a difficult connection with the ground plane and a retaining wall that was to make the areaway behind the basement. We settled for the mutation of the sloping extension of the ground plane to a 'tail' that could be supported on a pier (as a conventional porch roof might be). We sacrificed our 'poetic' interpretation of the meadow rising: the tail now required a very disjunctive step up on to it. Making the roof deck of timber required steel beams to produce the spans. The steel beams would bear on paired masonry piers, dimensioned to make smaller vertical cores which could be interpreted to locate doors, plumbing stacks and 'adhesive' surfaces to which other items might gravitate. We made the steel beams with tubes as they more easily reconciled the sloping roof plane to the masonry bearings which, in turn, were generally formed as 'U'-forms in plan to give buttressing stability and to make recesses that, like the masonry piers, are interpretable for storage and for benches spanning between the arms of the 'U'.

The steel beams and their supporting frameworks were welded away from the site. Bringing them into their places by crane was a memorable event, as barn-raisings must have been, their size and complexity being in contrast to the small elements of conventional domestic construction. Their memorability was confirmed when, much later, and by accident, we discovered details of traditional Kwakiutl and Haida houses where not only large cedar tree beams bear on lintels supported by two doorposts but, in their 'two-beam' houses, two parallel beams bear directly above the two central door posts forming a central nave and supporting wider, flanking aisles.[iv] Within our smaller central space are located a stove against one of the pier units, on axis with the two doors, its flue passing between the paired steel tubes.

82

ii Ontario barns have a masonry base which houses livestock for the winter as well as for the daily routines of milking. Above this is a framed building - a warehouse - for storing hay for winter-feeding. 'Gangways' or ramps allow carts to be pulled up on to the upper floor so that hay bales may be unloaded and stored. The ramp has an obvious utility. More important, it has slightly less obvious poetry. It suggests a gentle 'change of state' as it encourages a detachment from the earth's worldly state all the while remaining in the world. Latent within its form is the potential for 'outreach' if not 'uplift.' Gaston Bachelard has suggested that to sleep in the branches of a tree is to be close to Heaven while being anchored to the earth by its trunk and roots. Children can interpret their play in tree houses as a detachment from the adult world while remaining securely rooted in it by the tree. We also remembered the moonviewing platform in Kyoto as an agent for daydreaming, if not 'uplift'.

iii Soon after we began construction we read The Refinement of America, by Prof. R. Bushman. Bushman explains the development of the middle class and its determination to acquire the 'aristocratic' manners of gentility and refinement. The hallmark of refinement is the elimination of all evidence of work being, and having been, done from daily life. According to Bushman, enthusiasm for things refined is fuelled by snobbery. Hopefully, our enthusiasm for work-a-day things is not infected by inverted snobbery or a *nostalgie de la boue* (to which those who would go to cottages are all too prone).

iv P. Nabokov-R. Easton, Native American Architecture, Oxford University Press, New York, 1989.

v Spazio e Società, no. 78, 'Time Rebuffed', pp. 24-35.

The concrete block piers led us to think of the masonry elements of the basement and its associated piers rising from and being of the ground juxtaposed with lightweight curved perimeter screen walls and the roof. We acquired unsolicited and remarkable overhangs at each corner where the curved walls receded. Even better, due to the sloping ground plane, each overhang was proportionally different: the one on the southwest corner was twice the height of the one on the northeast corner. (The northeast overhang was to become a porch over the entrance ramps; at the northwest shelters the steps down to the basement and undercroft while the southwest acts as a two-storey porch between the low ceilinged undercroft and the open field to the south).

The value of an extended construction period - we were trying to build the house ourselves within the limits of our abilities, relying on help from professionals and friends for those aspects of the construction that required skills and manpower we lacked - is having time to rethink most things. We found that rethinking sets up a chain reaction. For example, we had bought curved, corrugated galvanized steel sections (for grain storage silos) in order to experiment with the 'roll top' roofs and to match their radius. Changing the roof made the corrugated steel pieces redundant and they were assigned to the stockpile of materials, with the hope that there was a future for them. Indeed there was: sometime later, we realized they could be used, half-buried and filled, to make a newel-like drum around which steps might spiral to take up the level difference and give access, under the north-west overhang, to the basement and undercroft.

Improbably, perhaps, our silo-become-newel allows a comparison with Picasso's *Head of a Bull*. Through the sculpture, all we know of bulls collides with all we know of bicycles and neither will ever be quite as they were. It is the classic formulation of a joke: two or more disconnected things, a gent and a banana skin, interact with momentarily shocking and therefore memorable consequences. Each has acquired an indelible association with the other, forever complicating our perception of them both. (Admittedly, Picasso's *Head of a Bull* is a good joke while our newel isn't much of one at all). Since Picasso made his sculpture in 1943, we may have become somewhat blasé, if not condescending, about 'found objects' - perhaps we have suffered too much driftwood. Nevertheless, all things, in one way or another, are to be found and, on being found, invite us to domesticate them as, by the process of association, we make the unfamiliar familiar. (Or, as Picasso does, the familiar is made less so).

Writing elsewhere,[v] I broached the idea that 'associational thinking' might be better recognized as an intrinsic part of 'the design process'. I mentioned Jean-Paul Gaultier, the fashion designer, had created a perfume with a trace of the smell of fingernail polish (or polish remover) in it. He said he wanted to snag early memories of using make up and being 'feminine' believing that those memories would confirm the desirability of the new perfume and, of course, snag new customers. It is the idea of snagging memories that is important. Latent in all things is the snagging of other things.

83

vi P. Prangnell, 'The Friendly Object', Harvard Educational Review, vol. 39, no. 4, 1969, pp. 36-41.

I have said that we admire farm buildings and literally willed an association between them and our house by its forms and its materials. These associations are direct: we assume visitors get them. Also willed are associations we have made with particular things and events - our personal libraries of images - which are, perhaps, less directly 'got'. For example, for a period during the construction, having to use a wheelchair made us rethink the entrance we had proposed to the loft level from the grassed, sloped roof.

Because of the wheelchair incident, we changed the entrance to the main floor and put in a ramp to it, rather than steps. In spite of the wheelchair, we didn't want to evoke the associations that 'handicapped access' brings to mind. We wanted our ramp to be a discrete thing - as ships' gangways and stairs wheeled to airplane doors are - bridging two separate domains. We thought of boat launching ramps and the beauty of their surface meeting the water's edge and going on down under it. Our ramp has its top edge shy of the doorway and its bottom edge partially hidden by the gravel stones that lap over it. We paved it with a local stone that, when cut and wet, shows wave-like marbling. For us, these associations are direct. We would be delighted if the ramp unconsciously snagged similar associations for visitors.

Our general admiration of agricultural and industrial buildings led us to work on the designs as an accretion of disparate pieces in two ways: first, by showing wherever possible the volumes of discrete spaces; second, by revealing, wherever possible, the structure of the construction. Almost as a badge of honour, and risking rusticity, if not gawkiness, we wanted to avoid those aspects of genteel redefinement that may be represented by shiny, smooth surfaces and an absence of all signs of work being done. For all this, I hesitate to use the term 'democratic'. Yet by recognizing all the constituent pieces of a construction as being in a peer relationship, not only with each other but with the inhabitants of that construction, it is tantamount to being so.

Many years ago I wrote about 'Friendly Objects'. [vi] They are those things we have gathered by us to improve, to make more comfortable and agreeable, our physical and, often, emotional existence. If, for a moment, we think of pets and our varying relations and attitudes towards them, it may be possible, going from animate to inanimate, to see all the artifacts of existence in much the same way. Pets reflect the gamut of human attitudes: dependence and companionship, snobbery and ostentation, affection and intimidation, maintenance and neglect. We treat things in much the same way: we look after them or not; some respond to our care while others do not; some appear as trophies while others are banished.

We would like to think our house is a gathering of many such friendly objects and pieces. Not only the obvious set pieces - the cabinets, for example - but also the components of the construction: the discrete pieces of the steel structures, each wall and each ceiling, each door and each window, each stair flight, the supports for shower heads, the supports for workshops, the supports for balustrade panels and the panels themselves. The vertical steel elements are embellished with coloured glass inserts, strategically placed to catch passing eyes, for a moment drawing attention to themselves. We live with them all and they give us space between them for our business of living amongst them. Not unlike 'going native' (as we say of those who go to live among indigenous peoples and have difficulty coming back) among all the bits of building, the topography, the vegetation, that form an inclusive environment.

By allowing each object its own independence, new geometries appear liberated from the orthogonal geometry of drafting, or the 'inherent' or extended geometry of conventional construction. As goat paths do, being a path of desire worked out in a goatish manner within its environment. For example, we extended the stone hearth around the stove as a path to the basement stair, knowing it would be the way firewood would be brought in from its outdoor storage. Less direct than this angled path is the dormer we put over the washbasin in the *cabanon* space. It works as a sort of light funnel and a hood over the oven. It sits astride the dual-tube structure, anchored to one tube while the other tube runs free through the interior space of the angled funnel or hood.

Time, inevitably, became a major element in the process we found ourselves committed to: we've spent twelve years making our house. Of course, we are in good company! Ferdinand Cheval spent some 33 years building his Palais Ideal (Spazio e Società, no. 27). The Palais is, I believe, as intimate a building as, according to Bachelard, mollusks' shells and birds' nests are. Cheval made it himself for himself. It appears to be worked from the inside out. Describing it, I drew an analogy to the poet Charles Olsen's concept of 'Projective Verse.' Olsen said, among other things, 'It is a matter, finally, of objects, what they are, what they are inside a poem, how they got there, and, once there, how they are to be used.' ... Every element in an open poem (the syllable, the line, as well as the image, the sound, the sense) must be taken up as participants in the kinetic of the poem just as solidly as we are accustomed to take what we call the objects of reality; and that these elements are to be seen as creating the tensions of a poem just as totally as do those other objects create what we know as the world. 'A poem', he wrote, 'is energy transferred from where the poet got it, ... by way of the poem itself to, all the way over to, the reader.'

Rejecting 'print-bred' verse for 'projective' verse, Olsen said 'what projective verse teaches, is, this lesson, that the verse will only do in which a poet manages to register both the acquisitions of his ear and the pressure of his breath.' Which is, in part, to say that the poet anticipates the in-and-out of our breathing as we speak his poem and understand that he breathes much as we do. When Le Corbusier observed that 'it is always life that is right' he came close to suggesting that architecture, like 'projective' verse reflecting the rhythms of in-and-out breathing, will reflect the ins-and-outs of life - if we give it time.

Verse, after all, is no more than speech made memorable.

Community

Here the cultures of design and private lives forge values and shared meanings that directly contribute to what can only be called community.

7 It is in this context that the thoughtless transposition of private suburban comforts to the countryside appears so unnecessary and ultimately so callous.

With the vast majority of Canadians now inhabiting some form of urban domain, conventional stereotypes of canoes, northern lights and campfires may be inexorably drifting apart from our lives as lived. In the midst of projects that are singular and held tightly to the scale of family and friends, the suggestion is often still present of how these private sensibilities might extend to a larger community of interests. The breadth of common experience already noted surely indicates the potential for a sense of collective value, yet the specific inclinations of the projects also intimate public practice at another scale.

As much as a sense of community is reliant upon a set of shared values, it may also be conjured through the shared experiences in which values are forged. While each of us may recall a different landscape, a different shelter and a different domestic realm in our response to the cottage theme, it is almost certain that we will share in the clarity and significance of that response.[7]

In projects by *Shim-Sutcliffe Architects* and *Brian MacKay-Lyons Architects* the potential for a sensibility borne of modest and domestic circumstances to embrace collective activities is given credible - indeed *remarkable* - expression. There exists a kind of seamlessness in an extrapolation by both architects of the virtues of individual houses into these community structures that alludes to continuity between the projects of building and landscape more generally.

Moorelands Camp Dining Hall and Kitchen

SHIM-SUTCLIFFE ARCHITECTS

The northern Ontario landscape is filled with lakes, remote islands and peninsulas heavily laden with pine trees and strewn with large rocks. It is on one of these peninsulas that Moorelands Camp is located.

Accessible only by crossing Lake Kawagama by boat, the non-profit camp is an annual summer destination for economically disadvantaged children from Toronto and its surrounding areas who are offered a chance to experience the wilderness for a few weeks. The new dining hall provides an opportunity to embody the spirit of the camp in a structure that could crystallize the collective aspirations for the building and for the children that it serves.

The dining hall creates a luminous clearing in the woods. Twelve glue-lam trusses combine with small scale dimensioned lumber and light steel elements to create a simple 'wooden tent'. The compression members of the truss are made of a continuous line of 2 x 4's to form a structural truss 'lantern'. The main space is 36 feet wide and 100 feet long. The roof extends beyond the exterior building wall by two bays to provide a large covered outdoor porch for camp activities. The natural cedar siding on the exterior is detailed to weather graciously over the decades and mellow with time.

The exposed structure creates a light and luminous interior that glows with the life of the camp.

The exposed structure creates a light and luminous interior that glows with the life of the camp.

The dining hall is used heavily during the summer months and is closed down for the rest of the year. Wooden *brises-soleil* provide summer shading and fold down to facilitate winter closing. A motorized greenhouse glazing system runs the length of the building along the roof ridge, bringing light into the building and providing flow-through ventilation.

Brian MacKay-Lyons Architect Ltd.

'Imagine flying over the bones of a ghost village on the edge of the world.'

Ghost Research Lab is an ongoing project, initiated in partnership with Dalhousie University, in which two-week design-build workshops result in an accumulation of constructions accompanied by the ephemera of construction and community. The project is designed to promote the transfer of architectural knowledge through direct experience, project-based learning with an emphasis on issues of landscape, material culture and community.

Directed by Brian MacKay-Lyons, this educational initiative takes place each summer on the ruins of a 400-year-old village at the MacKay-Lyons farm on the Nova Scotia coast. The project selects a unique component annually in pursuit of ongoing research experiences and the emerging collective identity of the work. At the session's conclusion, the completed structures serve as the venue for a community gathering, featuring local musicians who help interpret the cultural history of the site. Invited architectural theorists and practitioners contribute to the overall research component of the workshop.

Ghost Lab offers evidence of a collective expression of the cultural ecology of the region, building upon the framing and shipbuilding traditions of the area.

Ghost Lab offers evidence of a collective expression of the cultural ecology of the region, building upon the framing and shipbuilding traditions of the area.

95

MacKay-Lyons

Barns, sheds and lobster traps serve as precedents for each session's final design, which moves to the building stage with the help of professional contractors. Participants build wood-frame pavilions suggestive of 18th century follies, relying as well on light and wind to animate the structure.

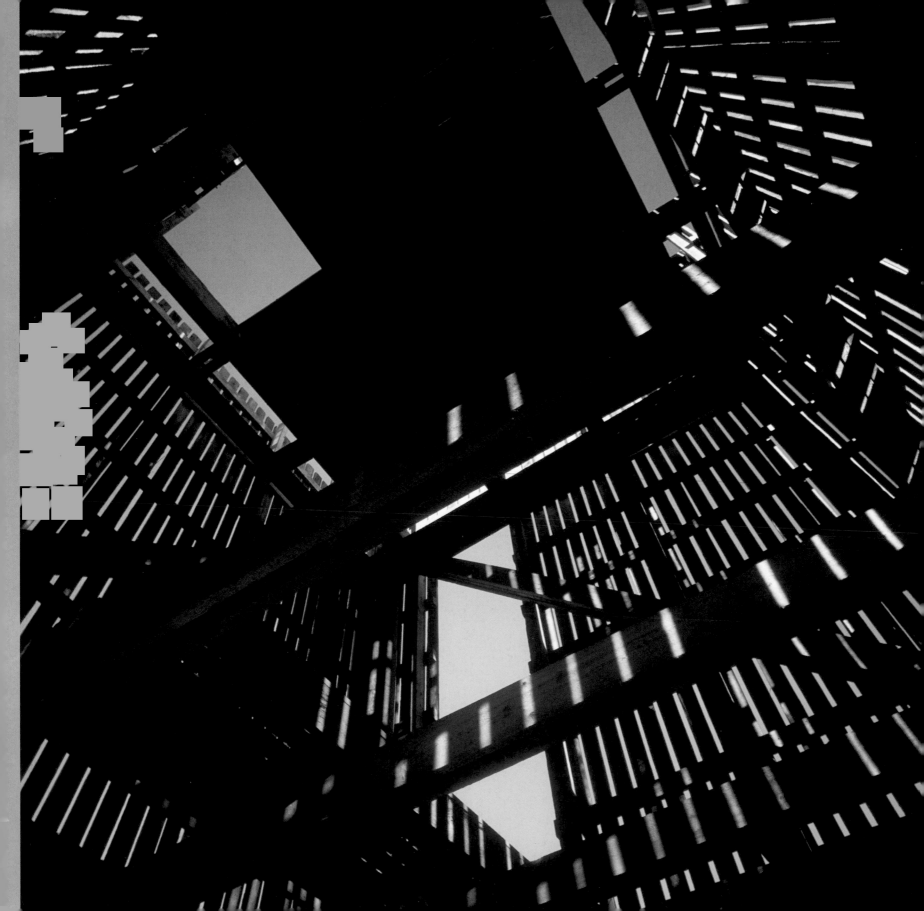

Closing

The work invites a consideration of the sensibilities that will continue to inform future designs on the Canadian landscape. Is there a point beyond which the synthetic framing of our landscape experience overwhelms that experience beyond recognition? How might longstanding habits of modestly inhabiting our landscape find contemporary expression and resolve?

102

The theme of holiday house quite naturally draws to it associations of varied and distinct pleasure. It would be fair, however to balance this project's positive virtues with an acknowledgement that much current practice simply transplants suburban comforts to the countryside - SUV and all. Cabin and camp channeled through Ralph Lauren, these outsized 'recreational properties' arrive [8] with casual concern for issues of geography, local history or the consequences to local economies.

8 Clearly this inclination is encouraged and even mandated by the demands of planning and building regulations being indiscriminately disposed: responsible not only for double glazing and 'proper' construction but often insisting upon stylistic and material conformity as well.

The work collected here bears witness to resistant strains of design and cultural desire, and challenges an ethos that in many regions aggressively threatens the very landscape qualities it professes to enjoy. While hardly comprehensive, this work represents intentions of clients and designers that are as varied as they are forceful. Thematic connections between projects have been directly acknowledged and other overlapping relationships are certainly here to be discovered, bearing witness to the potential depth and substance of the theme.

While the focus on these houses is alluring in its appeal to the familiar, it might be useful in conclusion to emphasize that central to the cabin, cottage and camp project is a concern for social practice as much as a fascination with the artifact of the house itself.

As well, the extent to which attributes of cabin and cottage life might find presence in an emerging urban reality presents intriguing possibilities. Last summer's collection of seashells set alongside the bath or snapshots lingering on the fridge door... the souvenir has always performed an essential role in reinforcing the special qualities of the cottage experience. Yet how else might qualities aligned with local, seasonal habits come to inform contemporary urban forms of domestic life? How might these collective memories be granted spatial presence? [9]

While the pleasures of visiting a 'home away' are unquestionably privileged, they have for some time been an extraordinarily common privilege. Insofar as they represent one small component of a collective national identity they invite no less than our thoughtful and critical consideration.

9 In our current embrace of 'loft' patterned condominiums might we find the requisite cultural antecedent as readily in the lives of cabin and cottage as in the domestic colonization of industrial buildings? Canada: a new domestic wilderness...

Project Plans

All plans are shown at a scale of $^1/_{16}$" = 1'- 0" with north, where applicable, to the top of the page.

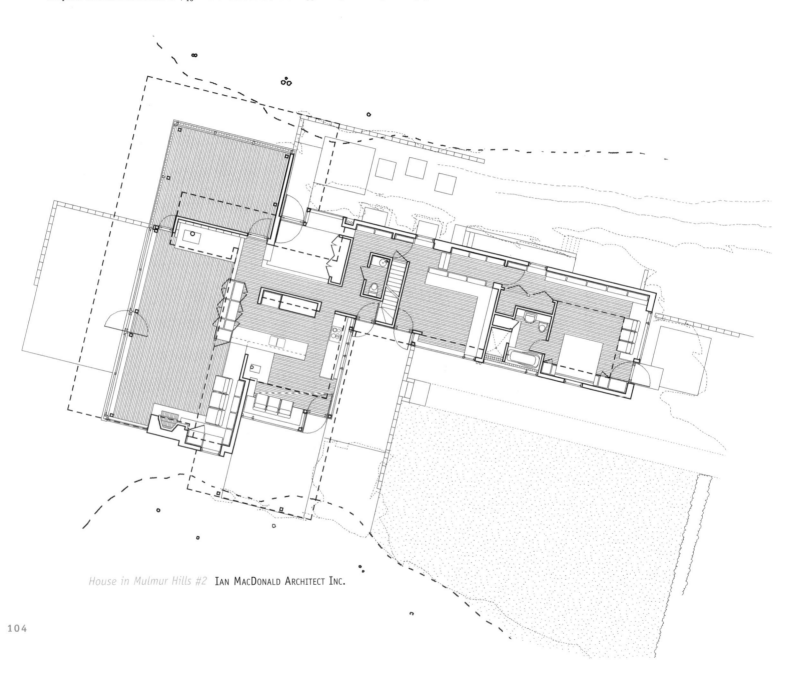

House in Mulmur Hills #2 IAN MACDONALD ARCHITECT INC.

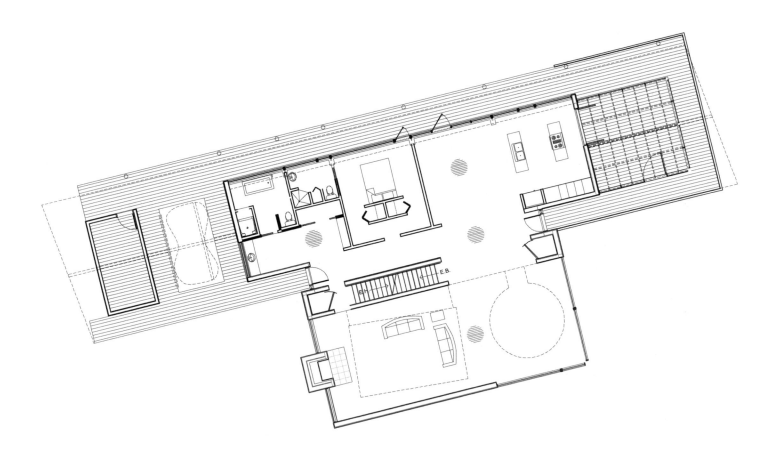

Residence 'Les Abouts' PIERRE THIBAULT ARCHITECTE

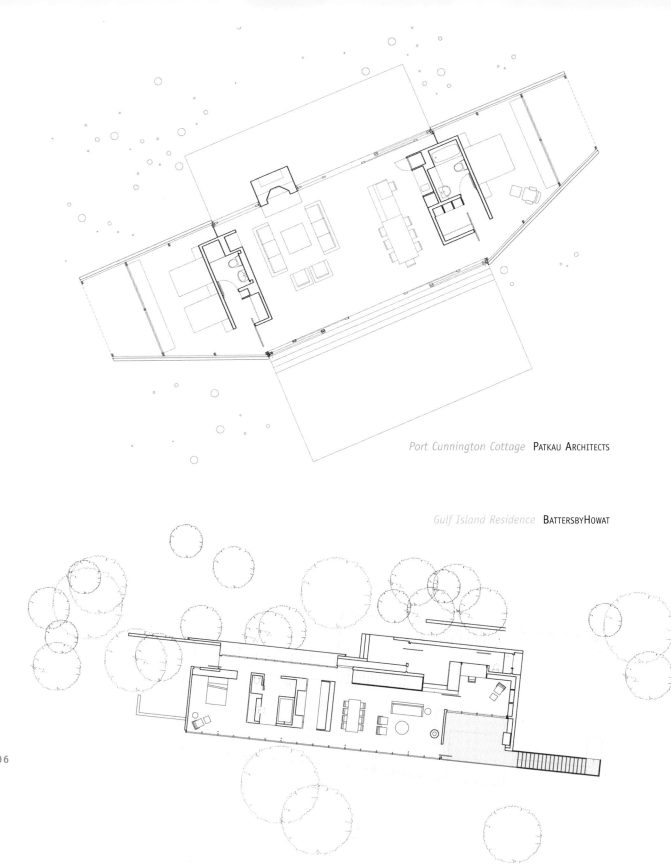

Port Cunnington Cottage PATKAU ARCHITECTS

Gulf Island Residence BATTERSBYHOWAT

106

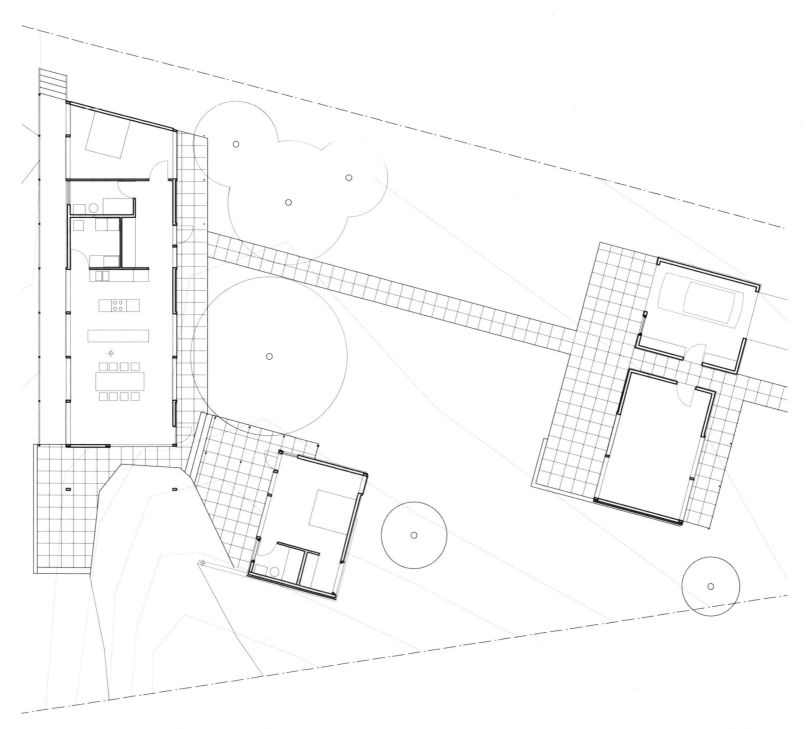

House in Naramata FLORIAN MAURER ARCHITECT INC.

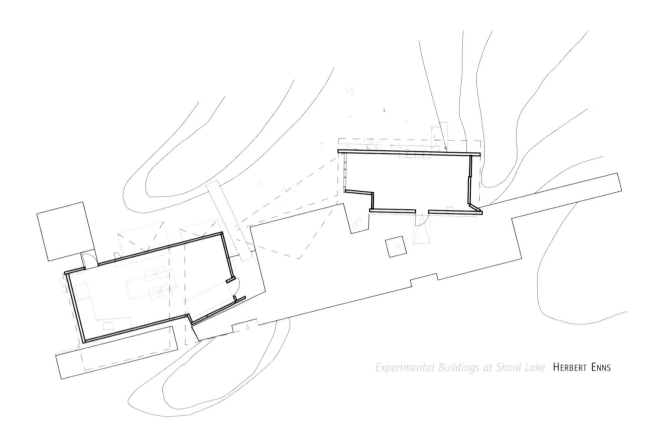

Experimental Buildings at Shoal Lake HERBERT ENNS

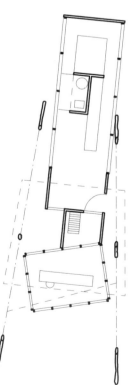

Habitats Légers PIERRE THIBAULT ARCHITECTE

108

La Petite Maison du Weekend Patkau Architects

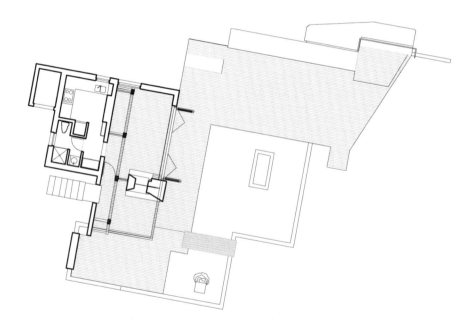

Ravine Guest House and Reflecting Pool Shim-Sutcliffe Architects

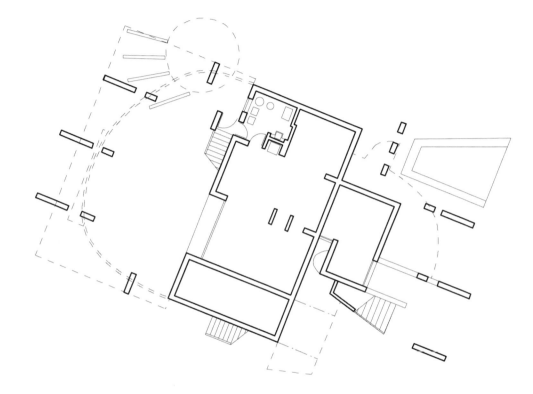

Hobby House PETER PRANGNELL AND ANTHONY BELCHER

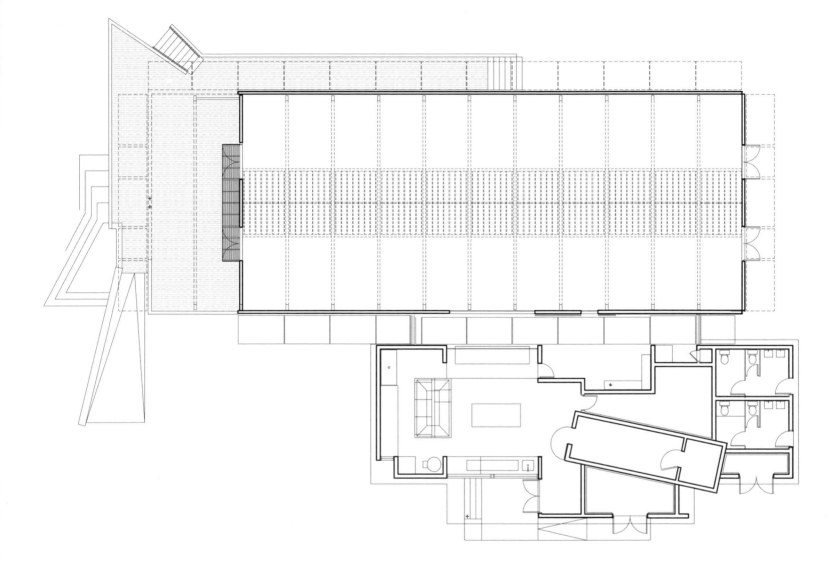

Moorelands Camp Dining Hall and Kitchen SHIM-SUTCLIFFE ARCHITECTS

Credits

BattersbyHowat

www.battersbyhowat.com

Established in 1996, BattersbyHowat was founded as a partnership between David Battersby and Heather Howat.

The practice is conceived as a collaborative studio endeavour, working from a background of combined degrees in architecture, landscape architecture, and interior design. The firm has been involved in varying scales of privately commissioned work - residences, gardens, art galleries, showrooms, office interiors, and custom furniture. The practice pursues an architectural expression that embodies a spirit of contemporary living that is modest and without pretense.

Peter Cardew Architects

www.cardew.ca

Established twenty years ago, Peter Cardew's practice has been responsible for projects that have received international recognition through numerous awards and publications.

The architecture he has been responsible for covers a wide range of building types including schools, exhibition buildings, housing, office buildings, libraries, art galleries, and private residences. The projects undertaken by the firm are generally of a more institutional/cultural nature where the complexities of programme demand more innovative and creative solutions than those associated with repetitive commercial projects.

Peter has taught as an adjunct professor at the University of British Columbia, the University of Calgary, Washington State University and has lectured extensively in North and South America, Europe and Australia.

Saturna Island House

British Columbia
Peter Cardew with David Scott, Angie Jim and Rob Grant: drawings by Peter Cardew with model by Derek Kaplan and David Scott

Herbert Enns

www.umanitoba.ca

Herbert Enns is Professor in the Department of Architecture at the University of Manitoba. His practice consolidates his dual interests in teaching and building, and focuses on creativity and design as applied not only to the façade of a building, but to human relationships as well.

Enns is a regional correspondent and frequent contributor to Canadian Architect, and recent activities as critic and curator include projects that consider the prints of Joseph Albers and recent work by architect Toyo Ito.

PHOTOGRAPHY Thomas Fricke and Herbert Enns.

Ian MacDonald Architect Inc.

www.ima.ca

The firm of Ian MacDonald Architect Inc. was established in Toronto in 1984. The firm's work includes projects of varied scale and use with an emphasis on residential work. The focus of the work has always been on developing legible, site specific architecture that articulates a clear idea and sense of place. Responsive siting strategies, spatial richness, and honestly articulated materials all within a well crafted, modern vocabulary contributes to the realization of this focus.

Attitudes and ideas that are employed on smaller residential projects find expression in larger scale work as well.

Brian MacKay-Lyons Architect Ltd.

www.bmlaud.ca

The Halifax-based office of Brian MacKay-Lyons has developed a consistent body of work based on a modern regionalist architectural language, which combines the use of archetypal forms with local building practices.

Founded in 1985, the firm focuses on houses, public buildings and urban design commissions, which have accumulated to form an extensive and consistent body of work in the Maritimes. MacKay-Lyons' work has been characterized as one of resistance, in which the act of rebuffing the elements becomes paramount to the design itself, with cladding pulled hard to the ground and windows cut out like portholes.

PHOTOGRAPY Jamie Steeves and Stephen Evans

Florian Maurer Architect Inc.

www.florianmaurer.com

Florian Maurer has been practicing since 2003 from a base in British Columbia's Okanagan, following a three-year sojourn in Italy where he worked on aid projects in Romania as well as local projects in Northern Italy. Prior to establishing his current practice, Maurer was senior principal of Florian Maurer Architect Inc. and Maurer Kobayashi Architects Ltd. in Whitehorse.
The architect's designs are developed through a Form Follows Physics process, which emphasizes a thorough manipulation of structural, functional and technical ideas.

PHOTOGRAPY Stuart Bish

Patkau Architects

www.patkau.ca

Patkau Architects, founded in 1978, is a Vancouver-based practice led by principals John Patkau, Patricia Patkau and Michael Cunningham and associates David Shone, Peter Suter and Greg Boothroyd.
A series of early houses, schools, libraries and galleries helped to establish the firm's design reputation and was followed by success in a number of international design competitions. Since then, the work in the office has expanded to include a wide variety of building types varying in scale from gallery installations to urban planning, from houses to major urban libraries, from glassware and fur-

niture design to research into sustainable practice and the future of educational technologies.
While circumstances of the work change, the firm's interest remains constant: to explore the depth of the discipline, understanding it as a critical cultural act that engages the most fundamental desires and aspirations.

Peter Prangnell and Anthony Belcher

ajbpp@sympatico.ca

Peter Prangnell and Anthony Belcher have worked together on a number of projects - building the house in Euphrasia occupied them, weekends and holidays, for fifteen years or so.
Peter Prangnell taught design at the AA, Harvard GSD, Columbia, and, as a visitor, at MIT, Berkeley and Washington University, St. Louis. In the late 1960s he introduced, with John Andrews and others, the 'New Programme' curriculum in the Department of Architecture at the University of Toronto. He has contributed many articles to Giancarlo De Carlo's magazine, Spazio e Società and Canadian Architect.
Anthony Belcher established his own practice - Anthony Belcher Architect - in 1995 undertaking residential and garden designs, several of which have been featured in Canadian House & Home.

Shim-Sutcliffe Architects

www.shim-sutcliffe.com

Brigitte Shim and Howard Sutcliffe are partners as well as collaborators. They have created a firm and a life around their shared passion for architecture, landscape and furniture. Their studio is located in Toronto, Canada. The city's diversity and ethnicity make it a vital metropolis reflective of both global and North American sensibilities. Their work references both the city and its landscape within the urban core of Toronto and the many particular landscapes around it. The studio works in an intense and probing way, sharing ideas through drawings, models and discussion with the numerous remarkable clients who have put their faith in them over the past decade.

The studio as well as its two partners has received numerous awards for their work, which has been published widely. Howard Sutcliffe was the first recipient of the Ronald Thom Award for Early Design Achievement awarded by the Canada Council for the Arts. Brigitte Shim is a professor at the University of Toronto Faculty of Architecture, Landscape and Design and has held visiting positions at the Ecole Polytechnique Federal de Lausanne, at Yale University and at Harvard University's Graduate School of Design.

Moorelands Camp Dining Hall and Kitchen

Lake Kawagama, Dorset, Ontario
Brigitte Shim and Howard Sutcliffe with Jason Emery Groen: presentation drawings by Min Wang
Client: Downtown Churchworkers Association
Structural Engineer: Dave Bowick, Blackwell Engineering
Builder: Gord McLean and crew / Barry Chumbly, Site Coordination

PHOTOGRAPHY Michael Awad, James Dow

Pierre Thibault Architecte

www.pthibault.com

Through environmentally incisive responses to the needs of clients in urban, regional and wilderness settings, Pierre Thibault's Quebec City practice has been distinguishing itself since 1988. The firm has been recognized both for innovative design and intelligent responses to client needs, with an emphasis in establishing a dialogue between architecture, art and landscape.
Continuing research is borne out in realized projects including landscape interventions, large and small-scale cultural and residential projects. The interrelation of landscape, site history and cultural context allows for the development of distinctive solutions rich with meaning, atmosphere and heightened sensory awareness. Pierre Thibault Architecte has received numerous prizes, including the Governor General's Award for Architecture, the Progressive Architecture Awards, Canadian Architecture awards, and the Prix de Rome.

Residence 'Les Abouts'

Saint-Edmond-de-Grantham, Québec
Pierre Thibault

PHOTOGRAPHY Alain Laforest

Habitats Légers

St. Gervais, Quebec
Pierre Thibault with Eric Thibodeau

Acknowledgements

This publication and its related exhibition and symposia represent extensive and sustained contributions by many. Thanks are due to Brigitte Desrochers for her formative support on behalf of the Canada Council for the Arts; Jana Tyner and the School of Architecture at the University of British Columbia for unflagging support throughout the process; Greg Bellerby and the support staff from Emily Carr Institute of Art and Design; Dimiter Savoff, Elisa Gutiérrez and Carlos Mendes for their contributions to both exhibition design and publication; Brian Billingsley for formatting the plans for the publication.

The significance of contributions from all participants in the project should as well be noted. Both time and invaluable advice were forthcoming in the midst of challenging professional lives.

Finally, gratitude should be extended to the clients of these distinguished projects. In their hands rests the future expression of this cultural habit called out here as Cabin, Cottage and Camp.

Chris Macdonald

Canada Council   Conseil des Arts
for the Arts   du Canada

On the Pacific I have kidnapped an island
from a rich dog-salmon
and take it home with me
park it beside the bed
and now I dream of islands
in a spring of wild roses
and write another poem
in this enchanted country

Al Purdy, from 'Home'